Mr
Appl

When the railway line was closed down, Mr Bubbus, the village station master, suddenly found himself out of a job. He missed the trains, and time seemed to pass very slowly, until the day his friend Mr Deggas's little girl found a steam engine called Forester abandoned in an old siding. But Sir Benjamin Bathbun was interested in steam engines too, and as soon as he knew about Forester, things started to go wrong. Joan Drake lives in South Wales and is the author of several books for younger children. Val Biro's witty illustrations accompany this appealing story.

Mr Bubbus and the Apple-green Engine

Joan Drake

Illustrated by Val Biro

Beaver Books

First published in 1971 by
Brockhampton Press Limited
(now Hodder & Stoughton Children's Books),
Salisbury Road, Leicester, England

This paperback edition published in 1977 by
The Hamlyn Publishing Group Limited
London · New York · Sydney · Toronto
Astronaut House, Feltham, Middlesex, England

ISBN 0 600 36275 2

Printed in England by Cox and Wyman Limited,
London, Reading and Fakenham
Set in Monotype Times

Contents

1	Bad news	9
2	The discovery	17
3	Grand opening	26
4	An offer	36
5	Robbed!	44
6	The first clue	53
7	Ambrose to the rescue	61
8	The end of the story	69

For Robert and Elizabeth Evans

Chapter One

Bad news

The village, a cluster of little cottages and houses around the church and the inn, clung to the side of a hill. Below, green fields gently sloped towards the bay, where the yellow sand met the shimmering sea. The railway ran along the edge of the bay and a winding lane led from the village to the station.

Mr Bubbus was the station-master. He was also the man who sold the tickets, the porter, the ticket collector and the left-luggage man. In the ticket office, three hats hung on hooks in a row. While Mr Bubbus sold tickets, saying briskly, 'Two singles to London,' or 'One and a half return to Liverpool,' he did not wear a hat. When he had dealt with his travellers, Mr Bubbus hastily donned his ticket collector's hat and rushed to the platform gate, ready to punch holes in the tickets. After the train left, Mr Bubbus put on his porter's hat as he sorted the parcels and luggage.

So you can see, he was a very busy man and didn't have much time to wear his station-master's hat. This he put on when an important person came to the village, which wasn't very often. Or when he had a few moments to spare. Then he strolled up and down the platform, hands behind his back, admiring the little station he kept so neat and tidy, and feeling well pleased with the world.

Mr Bubbus knew all the boys and girls of the village. When they left the little school and set off for the big town school, Mr Bubbus, small, plump and jolly, was there to bundle them into the train . . . and to keep it waiting for latecomers if need be. He heard all their news and in his office was a collection of books and scarves and football boots that somehow seemed to be left behind.

Mr Bubbus found the winter rather quiet. He loved the summer which brought the crowds tumbling from the trains with their buckets and spades and swim-suits and beach-balls.

And when the last train of the day pulled out of the station, Mr Bubbus locked the doors and walked up the lane. He had a room in Mrs Boxer's house. She was very kind to him. She made him rice puddings and mended his socks. But secretly Mr Bubbus had one great wish.

It was for a little home of his own.

So the days went by, summer and winter, sunshine and rain. Until one morning the postman brought a letter for Mr Bubbus and the sad blow fell.

'*Dear Mr Bubbus* (said the letter)

We find very few people are using the railway, especially in the winter. Therefore we are closing the line and there will be no more trains from the town to the village. The station must close down. A bus service will take passengers to and from the town. We shall not be requiring your services any longer . . .' and so on and so on. It was signed by the railway people.

Mr Bubbus was in a dreadful state. He couldn't believe the news. He ran up the road to the house of his best friend Mr Deggas. He burst in to the kitchen. The Deggas family was breakfasting. Eight spoons stopped halfway to eight mouths and eight pairs of eyes gazed at him in astonishment.

'Mr Bubbus, my friend, what is it?' cried Mr Deggas leaping to his feet. Mr Bubbus told him. Too few people were using the trains. His station must close.

'*Close the station?*' echoed Mr Deggas in awful tones. 'We cannot allow such a thing. Something must be done. *At once.*'

Unlike Mr Bubbus, Mr Deggas was married and had seven children whose names he could never remember. Mr Deggas was very rich. No one knew exactly what he did. He shut himself in his room for an hour or so each day, came out for his elevenses saying, 'Aha, that's that,' and then went for a walk.

'I think he's in something called "socks and spares",' said Mrs Deggas vaguely. As long as she had money to buy biscuits and wellingtons and bandages and such for the family, she didn't worry her head about it.

Mr Bubbus had great faith in his friend. If anyone could help him, it was Mr Deggas. But this time it was Ambrose the eldest boy who had an idea.

'Let's have a march, a protest march,' he suggested.

'Yes, and a sit-down protest as well,' said his sister Poppy.

'What a good idea, whoever you are,' cried Mr Deggas. 'Of course, that is what we must do. Everyone does it these days.'

'All the village will want to join in when they hear the news,' added Ambrose.

'Yes, we'll march to the station with placards saying KEEP OUR STATION OPEN and OUR STATION MUST NOT CLOSE,' declared Mr Deggas. 'Then we'll sit down in front of the station and we won't move until they promise to keep it open.'

'But they won't see you,' said Mr Bubbus reasonably. 'I'm the only one there.'

'That's true. So you are,' agreed Mr Deggas. 'Very well, we'll march to London. We'll show them.'

Everyone in the village was angry when they heard the news and all were eager to join the Deggas march. As London was rather a long way off, they decided to go by train and march to the railway offices from there. Banners were painted in large letters saying HANDS OFF OUR STATION and CLOSE NEVER – TRAINS FOREVER. (Mr Tims the grocer made this up and he was very proud of it.)

At last the day arrived and Mr Bubbus bundled the marchers, bristling with placards and banners, into the carriages.

'Good luck,' he called as the train drew out. He spent the rest of the day worrying and wondering. He mixed up the parcels and kept putting the

wrong hat on his head. In the evening the last train came in, carrying the tired marchers home.

'Well, how did it go? What happened?' Mr Bubbus eagerly questioned them. 'What did they say?'

'I think we did rather well,' said Mr Deggas modestly. 'The railway people came out and listened to us and they promised to think the matter over very carefully.'

'Oh good,' sighed Mr Bubbus thankfully. 'I'm sure when they do, they won't close us down. Thank you, everyone, for your splendid help.'

'My poor feet,' groaned Mr Deggas. They went wearily home.

So, the railway people thought the matter over carefully and decided to close the village station after all. The sad day came when the last train left the station for the last time. The railway people were very kind. They made speeches about Mr Bubbus and his long service to the railway and they gave him a gold watch.

'Thank you very much,' said Mr Bubbus. He tidied the station and, taking his three hats, he locked the door and walked unhappily up the lane. He felt so miserable, he went to bed early. He put the three hats where he could see them on the chest of drawers. Two tears rolled down his cheeks.

'What shall I do now?' he wondered. 'I'm not old, well, not *very* old. What shall I do? There must be something for me.'

And at that moment a wonderful idea flashed into his head.

Chapter Two

The discovery

The Deggas family agreed that Mr Bubbus's idea *was* wonderful when he told them about it next day.

'I'm going to buy the station,' he announced. 'I'm going to turn it into a house and have my own little home.'

'Splendid, splendid. Allow me to buy the station for you,' said Mr Deggas grandly, being very rich.

'Oh dear me, no, thank you all the same. I have some money in the bank. I've been saving up for years for my own little home,' said Mr Bubbus quietly, being very independent.

So it was all decided and before very long with much coming and going, to-ing and fro-ing and signing of papers and visits to the bank, Mr

Bubbus became the proud owner of the village station.

The Deggas family offered to help and soon the station was transformed. Sawing and hammering, making doors here and windows there, fitting in cupboards and putting up shelves, papering and painting, how busy they were. They worked day after day, night after night. At home, Mrs Deggas whirred away on her sewing-machine, making curtains for the new house, and at last the day came when the curtains were up at the windows and everything was ready.

'Upon my word,' gasped Mr Bubbus, looking round the neat but empty rooms. 'I haven't any furniture to put in. I never thought of that.' He decided to go into town to buy some, but before he could turn around, the people from the village came down to the new house. One had a table she

didn't need any more, another had a comfy armchair, someone else a bookcase.

'How kind,' murmured Mr Bubbus. 'How very kind.'

In the end, the little house seemed to have everything it needed and all Mr Bubbus had to buy were a few pots and pans.

'Isn't that lovely?' said Mr Bubbus. 'I look around my little house and remember all my kind friends by the things they have given me.'

Mrs Boxer was sorry to lose Mr Bubbus but she decided to go and live with her sister, so that was very satisfactory.

The great day arrived when Mr Bubbus moved into his new home, which he called *Station House*.

'Not a very clever name,' he remarked. 'But just right.'

He invited all the Deggas family to tea and what a happy time they had. They wished Mr Bubbus long life and happiness in his new home and drank his health in tea and fizzy lemonade.

So Mr Bubbus began a new life. He cleaned his house and cooked his meals and he made a little garden in the old station yard.

But somehow, the days were long and Mr Bubbus was not truly happy. Something was wrong. Something was missing. What could it be? He had a talk about it with his friend Mr Deggas.

'I do miss the trains,' he said, looking sorrowfully at the railway lines now almost smothered with nettles and dandelions. 'I wish I could find something to do. I can't just sit and twiddle my thumbs.'

'Twiddle your thumbs!' laughed Poppy, who was standing by.

'Let's go for a walk,' suggested Mr Deggas, 'while we think about it.'

'Can I come too?' asked Poppy.

'Oh very well,' agreed her father.

The two friends set off together. They wandered along the footpath beside the old railway line. Poppy ran ahead, treading down the tall grass and making a way for them, for it was a very long time since anyone had used the overgrown path. It was a hot day in late summer. Bees hummed among the wild flowers which scented the air and, high above them, a lark sang in the blue sky.

'Now, let us think,' began Mr Deggas. 'What you need is some work to do, my friend.'

'Yes, I know, but what?' said Mr Bubbus.

'How about painting and decorating?' suggested Mr Deggas.

'Oh dear me, no, I've had enough of that in my own house,' declared Mr Bubbus at once.

'How about window-cleaning?' asked Mr Deggas.

'Oh dear me, no. I've no head for heights. I couldn't climb the ladder,' stated Mr Bubbus.

'How about . . .' Mr Deggas started to ask, when Poppy called from somewhere in the distance.

'Dad . . . dy, come and look.'

'Where is she?' said Mr Deggas gazing around. Poppy was nowhere to be seen. They followed the trail of flattened grass. It turned from the footpath to a small stile.

'She must be over there,' observed Mr Bubbus. The two friends clambered over and Mr Bubbus looked about.

'Well, well, well,' he exclaimed. 'The old railway siding. I haven't been here for years and years. I'd forgotten all about it.'

'So has everyone else it seems,' said Mr Deggas.

The rusty lines could hardly be seen beneath a covering of ferns and grass and weeds. Thick hawthorn hedges bulged on either side and ivy-covered trees overhung everything, making a dark green tunnel where the sun could not break through. No birds sang here and in the warm green stillness Mr Bubbus felt rather nervous. He clutched his friend's arm.

Poppy called again, her voice muffled. 'Come and look. Come *here*!'

'Where is that girl, whatever her name is?' said

Mr Deggas crossly. He strode up the line, Mr Bubbus following closely behind. And there, at the end of the siding, stood a shed. Old, falling apart, some of the roof missing, windows cobwebbed and broken, the door swinging on its rusty hinges. It seemed as if the brambles creeping over it were holding it together.

Poppy appeared in the doorway, red-faced and smudgy, but smiling.

'Oh, there you are,' puffed Mr Deggas. 'What's all the fuss about?'

'Look inside. See what I've found,' cried Poppy triumphantly.

Mr Bubbus and Mr Deggas peered into the dim shed.

'Upon my word!' gasped Mr Deggas.

'Bless my soul!' exclaimed Mr Bubbus.

There in the gloom, dirty and rusty, covered with inches of dust and layer upon layer of grey cobwebs, stood a little old steam engine.

'Why, it's an 0–4–0 goods locomotive,' cried Mr Bubbus excitedly. He rushed around the engine, poking here and prodding there. 'Look, here's the name. It's the old Forester. I remember her. Hard little worker she was.'

He rubbed away some dust with his sleeve.

'Here's her number, 1260. She must have been here for years and years. The railway people must have forgotten all about her.'

'Isn't she sweet,' said Poppy. 'I love her. Will she go, Mr Bubbus, do you think, or is she broken?'

'She is certainly in bad shape,' observed Mr Bubbus. 'After all, this engine is about sixty years old. But I declare, if she was cleaned up and oiled and everything, I'm sure she would be in working order.'

'They knew how to make engines in those days,' nodded Mr Deggas wisely.

'Oh yes indeed. She's a little beauty,' agreed Mr Bubbus, hopping on to the footplate, and becoming covered in cobwebs. 'I used to be an engine-driver many years ago. I know about steam engines. I love them. Diesels aren't the same, you know. These old steam engines really seemed to be alive, with the fires going and the steam puffing out. Ah, those were the days.'

'There,' said Mr Deggas suddenly. 'You wanted something to do. What about this engine? Couldn't you mend it and make it work again?'

'I believe I could. Oh, what a splendid idea,' breathed Mr Bubbus, his eyes shining at the thought.

'Keep you busy for many a day,' said Mr Deggas.

They closed the shed door, propping it up with a big stone.

'We won't tell anyone about it,' decided Mr Bubbus, as they made their way back. 'We'll keep it a secret. We don't want everyone from the village coming up here.'

'Now Poppy, remember that,' said her father. 'You can tell Ambrose and the twins and Peterkin but not the little ones. This is to be a Bubbus and Deggas secret.'

'Hooray,' cheered Poppy, skipping along. 'I love secrets.'

'What a splendid discovery. Well done, Poppy,' cried Mr Bubbus. 'Now we've found the engine I feel as happy as can be.'

He whistled gaily all the way home.

Chapter Three

Grand opening

Every day of the late summer a little procession could be seen making its way to the old siding. Autumn came and the leaves of the trees turned gold and red and brown then drifted down and buried the railway lines completely.

Winter arrived with howling winds and fog and rain and snow, but still they came – Mr Bubbus and Mr Deggas with Ambrose and Poppy, the twins Pansy and Posy and Peterkin, when they were not in school.

First of all they mended the old shed, cutting away the brambles, putting on a new roof, fixing windows and doors. While they worked, Mr Bubbus told them stories of the old days when he had been the driver of steam engines. How the children loved to hear of those days.

'Go on, Mr Bubbus,' begged the boys and girls. 'Tell us about when you were on the Royal Mail.'

'There we were,' Mr Bubbus would begin happily. 'The driver, that was yours truly, me, and Bert the fireman. Always together we were. Shovelling coal in, Bert was. You should have seen those fires. Roaring away. We sped through the night across the dark countryside, our flames and steam lighting up the sky with glowing red. Like some great black dragon we were, snorting fire and smoke. Ah, those were the days. Not like now. Diesels, pah, green caterpillars, that's all they are. No *character* like steam engines. I'm sorry for you children,' Mr Bubbus would end. 'Sorry you never knew the old steam engines. Now, they *were* engines.'

The children loved this story, especially the dragon bit. Their eyes shone as they listened.

'We *must* make this little old engine work,' they said to each other. 'We *must* see the fires and hear the steam and smell the smoke.'

So they started on the little old engine. Taking it apart, rubbing and greasing, oiling and painting, until at last, by spring, all put together again, the little engine stood gleaming and glistening in the shadowy shed.

How happy Forester was to have been found. For many years she had worked so hard, pulling heavy loads from one place to another. At first, when they left her in the old shed on the siding, she had been glad of the rest. But as week after week, month after month, year after year passed by, the little engine knew that everyone had forgotten her and this made her very sad.

But now, here she was, almost as good as new again.

'Oh, she's beautiful,' breathed Poppy admiringly. Indeed she was. A pretty apple-green with a shining brass heart bolted to her chimney and the name FORESTER in gold letters glowing on her side.

'Make her go, Mr Bubbus,' urged Pansy and Posy. 'Please make her go.'

'We'll need coal,' hesitated Mr Bubbus.

'And we must clear the line.'

'No problem,' said Mr Deggas. He borrowed a lorry and brought a load of coal, and the Deggas children cleared the line and helped carry buckets of water from a nearby brook.

Together they heaved and pushed the little engine from the shed. Mr Bubbus and Mr Deggas stoked her up and Mr Deggas offered to be fireman. The fire crackled and roared, the engine hissed and clouds of steam rose triumphantly into the air. Hardly daring to breathe, the Deggas family stood by the line.

'Right, here goes,' cried Mr Bubbus, pulling this and prodding that. 'Let's see what happens.'

'Shuff chuff, shuff chuff,' panted the engine.

Slowly, slowly the pistons began to move, the wheels began to turn and the little engine glided sedately down the line, clickety click, clickety clack.

'Hooray,' cheered the Deggas children wildly, skipping and jumping and running alongside the engine. 'Hooray, hooray.'

Mr Bubbus and Mr Deggas beamed happily from the footplate. Mr Bubbus stopped Forester, and Ambrose, Poppy, Pansy, Posy and Peterkin clambered aboard, excitedly squeezing into the small space.

'Hold tight,' cried Mr Bubbus. He blew the whistle 'Whoooo hooo'. Shuff chuff, shuff chuff, up and down the siding puffed the little old engine, up and down. Clickety clack went her wheels.

'It's great, it's smashing, it's super,' declared the Deggas children, quite agreeing it was the best ride they had ever had in their lives. When it was over they locked the engine safely in the shed and walked home, chattering all the way.

'The time has come,' announced Mr Deggas, 'to tell the others our secret.'

Soon the news was all over the village and everyone including Mr Tims's father, who was the oldest person in the village, and the Deggas baby who was the youngest, went to the old siding to 'Oh' and 'Ah' over the gleaming little engine.

And everyone wanted a ride.

This gave Mr Bubbus a wonderful idea.

'We'll open the railway line again,' he said excitedly. 'We'll have our own trips around the bay. That's what we'll do.'

'Splendid,' agreed Mr Deggas. 'We can take holiday-makers in the summer.'

'We'll need carriages,' warned Mr Bubbus.

'No problem,' declared Mr Deggas.

They went to the railway yards outside the town, and bought two shabby old railway coaches.

'Here we go again,' said Ambrose.

Once more everyone set to work, mending and putting to rights.

'Now we must paint them. What colour? Something very gay,' cried Mr Bubbus.

'Red,' thought Mr Deggas.

'Yellow,' suggested Ambrose.

'Black,' said Peterkin.

'Blue,' squeaked the twins.

'Let's use lots of colours with flowers and things,' said Poppy.

'That's it. That's what we want, something different,' nodded Mr Bubbus.

They bought tins of paint in every colour, pink and blue and orange and green and purple and red and yellow. Poppy, being very artistic, showed the others what she wanted and they began painting away.

The old carriages were soon transformed. Gay flowers blossomed up the sides and doors. Balloons and kites on strings wiggled up between the windows and birds and butterflies winged over the roofs.

'Beautiful, beautiful,' beamed Mr Bubbus when they were finished and Mr Deggas smiled fondly on his children.

Slowly, foot by foot, the line was cleared of weeds and grass and by Eastertime everything was ready. Easter Monday was chosen as the Great Day.

GRAND OPENING

THE BUBBUS AND DEGGAS RAILWAY CO

('That's short for Company,' said Mr Deggas knowledgeably.)

EASTER MONDAY

TRIPS AROUND THE BAY

Big notices were posted around the village and in the town.

Easter Monday dawned sunny and warm.

'Couldn't be better,' smiled Mr Bubbus, looking out from Station House.

By eleven o'clock crowds had gathered outside. The village band came swinging down the lane to the tune of 'Seventy-six Trombones'. As the band had only one trombone and that was played by Mr Tims's old father, it didn't sound quite right, but no one minded.

'Umpity-tump tump tump umpy umpity,' played the band, halting outside the station.

It had been decided that Poppy should perform the opening ceremony.

'After all,' said Mr Bubbus, 'Poppy found our engine and the decorations are her idea.'

So here was Poppy in her best pink party frock, splendid white socks and new hair ribbons, proudly surrounded by the Deggas family.

'Silence, please, quiet,' called Mr Deggas, and when everyone had stopped talking and shuffling about, Mr Bubbus made his speech.

'This is a happy day for us all,' he said. 'The old railway line is working again and I hope you will enjoy riding on our train. Thank you. I will now call upon Miss Poppy Deggas to open the Bubbus and Deggas Railway Co.'

Pink-cheeked, Poppy stepped forward. Mr Bubbus threw open his front door and everyone streamed through his hall, out of the back door and on to the platform, swept for the occasion and decorated with all the pot plants from the Bubbus and Deggas households. There on the line, quietly chuffing to herself, stood Forester, apple-green, brass gleaming, with her two gay carriages.

'How lovely! How gay! How pretty!' exclaimed the crowd.

A red ribbon stretched across the line in front of the engine.

'Now Poppy,' prompted Mr Bubbus.

Poppy stepped forward and snipped the ribbon with her mother's sewing scissors.

'I declare the Bubbus and Deggas Railway line is now open,' she cried in ringing tones.

'Hooray,' cheered the crowd, clapping hands and waving flags.

'The first ride *free* for everyone,' offered Mr Bubbus, putting on his driver's hat which he had bought especially for this day.

The passengers scrambled aboard and to the cheers of those left behind, Forester set off on her first trip. How happy she felt with her two pretty carriages behind her filled with gay excited people.

'This is better than pulling heavy loads of coal and ore,' she thought to herself, and her little boiler almost burst with pride as she steamed around the bay. On the footplate Mr Bubbus and Mr Deggas looked at each other and smiled.

'This is the life,' said Mr Bubbus, blowing the whistle 'Whoooo hoooo.'

'Couldn't be better,' said Mr Deggas, shovelling the coal.

Chapter Four

An offer

Beyond the village and far over the hill stood Bathbun Towers. It was a stately home built of grey stone, belonging to the noble Sir Benjamin Bathbun. Sir Benjamin spent all his time with his collection of engines. He had model engines from the tiniest matchbox size to one large enough to ride on and he had his own little railway line running around his vast overgrown garden. Between the apple trees it wandered, through the rhubarb and around the lake. In a big old barn, Sir Benjamin kept real engines, old ones, new ones, of every shape and size.

'I have the best collection of engines in the country,' he proudly declared. 'No, I tell a lie, in the *world*.'

But there was one engine missing from the

collection. Every now and again, Sir Benjamin would think about it and sigh.

'If only I had an 0–4–0 goods engine,' he'd say to himself, 'I'd be the happiest man on earth.'

Up and down the country he searched for one. In railway sheds and yards where old engines were taken to be broken up. A sad sight they were, dirty, rusty and forgotten. But there was never an 0–4–0 goods engine to be found.

One day, Sir Benjamin went into town to do some shopping. He saw a poster on a wall.

GRAND OPENING (he read)

THE BUBBUS AND DEGGAS RAILWAY CO

Sir Benjamin was very interested.

'I've never heard of the Bubbus and Deggas Railway Company,' he thought. 'I must go and see what they are about.' He climbed into his ancient Rolls-Royce.

'Thumper,' he said to his driver. 'Take me down to the bay at once.'

'Yessir,' said Thumper and away they went, up the hill and down, down, down, between the green fields, through the village and on down the winding lane to the station.

'Upon my word,' exclaimed Sir Benjamin Bathbun, astonished.

There was Station House, white paint sparkling,

dainty curtains at the windows, pink tulips nodding in the little garden. The front door stood wide open. A steady stream of mothers and fathers and boys and girls flowed through the hall of the house. Mr Deggas was busily selling tickets through the kitchen window and Mr Bubbus, on the platform, wearing his ticket collector's hat, was punching the tickets before his passengers climbed aboard the gaily painted carriages.

'Upon my word,' said Sir Benjamin again. 'Wait for me, Thumper,' he ordered, and joined the queue. He bought a ticket and walked on to the platform. He gazed with amazement at the flower-decked and ballooned carriages ... and then he saw the engine. Quietly chuffing to herself, waiting to begin her journey, small and shining, polished and trim.

Sir Benjamin nearly fainted away with shock. He could hardly believe his eyes.

'An 0–4–0 goods engine, number 1260 Forester. Oh, the beautiful, beautiful thing,' he whispered.

'All aboard,' shouted Mr Bubbus, slamming doors. Mr Deggas hurried from the kitchen, the whistle blew and they were off.

Shuff, chuff, shuff, chuff, gently they rolled round the bay. Clickety click, clickety clack. The train stopped several times to allow holiday-makers to jump down on to the sands with their picnic-baskets and towels and buckets and spades. The sea was blue as the sky above, sea-gulls whirled and screeched overhead, little yachts with sails of white and red bobbed on the shimmering water and children paddled and splashed where the creamy-edged waves lapped the golden sands.

But Sir Benjamin Bathbun had no eyes or ears for any of this. All he could think of was the sturdy little apple-green engine pulling them along.

'Shuff chuff,' she said. 'Shuff chuff,' as she curved gently ahead.

'I must have her,' thought Sir Benjamin. 'I *must* have her. I *must*.'

When she had rounded the bay, the little engine

went into reverse and pushed the carriages back again.

Chattering and laughing, the passengers left the station. Except for one person. Mr Bubbus and Mr Deggas smiled at each other.

'A good trip,' declared Mr Bubbus.

'Excellent,' agreed Mr Deggas. He glanced up the platform.

'Who is that looking at our engine?'

'I don't know,' said Mr Bubbus. He walked across and touched Sir Benjamin on his arm. 'Excuse me, sir, are you interested in old steam engines?'

'Indeed I am,' repled Sir Benjamin. 'Will you sell this one to me?'

'Sell our engine?' gasped Mr Bubbus.

'Sell Forester?' echoed Mr Deggas as if he couldn't believe his ears.

'Yes, I'd like to buy her. I'll give you a very good price,' offered Sir Benjamin Bathbun eagerly.

'Oh dear me, no. I'm sorry but we couldn't sell our engine, not at *any* price,' said Mr Bubbus firmly.

'Quite impossible,' stated Mr Deggas severely.

'Oh please sell her to me. I'll give you hundreds of pounds. *Thousands* of pounds,' pleaded Sir Benjamin wildly.

Mr Bubbus and Mr Deggas shook their heads.

'Forester is not for sale,' said Mr Bubbus flatly.

'I'll pay you anything, *anything* you like to ask,' cried Sir Benjamin desperately.

'No thank you. We do not wish to sell,' said Mr Bubbus with dignity. 'Come, Mr Deggas. Good afternoon, sir.'

They entered Station House and Sir Benjamin Bathbun was left champing with rage on the platform. He left the station purple in the face and jumped into his car.

'Take me home, Thumper,' he ordered, and sank back into his seat, sulking.

Mr Bubbus and Mr Deggas, peeping through the curtains, watched him go.

'What a funny man,' observed Mr Bubbus.

'He certainly wanted our engine very badly, didn't he?' said Mr Deggas. 'I wonder why?'

'I don't know,' replied Mr Bubbus. 'But he can't have her. We have such fun with our little train, don't we, Mr Deggas? We couldn't let Forester go.'

'Indeed we do. I've never enjoyed myself so much,' nodded Mr Deggas. 'Time for another trip?'

'Yes, here we go again,' said Mr Bubbus happily.

That evening, Sir Benjamin Bathbun tramped up and down his large room, up and down. He could think of nothing else but the little engine. In his mind he could see her shining and bright. He imagined her in the empty space in the big barn. He groaned.

Thumper brought him his cocoa and biscuits.

'Are you in pain, sir?' he asked.

'No, Thumper,' said Sir Benjamin, and told him the whole story.

'What can I do, Thumper?' he asked. 'I know they will never sell that engine to me. But I *must* have her.'

'Well, sir, we could just take it,' suggested Thumper.

'*Take it?*' gasped Sir Benjamin horrified. 'Do you mean . . . *steal* it, Thumper?'

'Don't say that, sir,' protested Thumper. 'We could just remove it, like.'

'That would be dishonest, Thumper,' said Sir Benjamin, who was not a bad man.

'You could leave them the money for it if you wanted to, sir, but we could just remove the engine when they weren't looking and save a lot of trouble, sir,' went on Thumper.

'How could we remove an engine, Thumper? The line only goes round the bay and up the siding,' pointed out Sir Benjamin. 'Be sensible.'

'There are other ways,' smiled Thumper. 'I've a wonderful plan, Sir Benjamin. Let me tell you about it.'

Sir Benjamin Bathbun listened to Thumper in amazement. At last he nodded his head.

'Very well, Thumper, go ahead,' he said. 'I must have that 0–4–0 engine. Tell me what to do.'

They sat making plans and plots far into the night.

Chapter Five

Robbed!

The last trip of the day was over. The crowds of holiday-makers had gone away and the station was quiet and deserted.

'Well done, little engine,' said Mr Bubbus proudly, rubbing Forester here and there with an oily rag. 'Time for a rest.'

They uncoupled the engine from the carriages and chuffed away up the siding to the shed.

Mr Bubbus and Mr Deggas said 'good night' to Forester and locked her safely in, then walked home together down the path.

'Come for supper?' invited Mr Deggas. 'Mrs Deggas is always glad to see you, you know.

'Very kind,' murmured Mr Bubbus. 'But I feel rather tired. I think I'll have an early night, thank you all the same.'

The two friends said 'good night' and 'see you in the morning' and 'sweet dreams' and 'sleep well' and things like that, and went on their way.

Mr Bubbus made himself some hot chocolate and a tomato sandwich and before very long he was tucked up in bed, fast asleep and snoring rather loudly.

'Snor-r-r-re, wheeeeee, snor-r-r-re, wheeeeee,' breathed Mr Bubbus, happily dreaming of steam engines speeding along miles and miles of shining rails under rainbow bridges to the stars.

The night was warm and still. The lights in the village went out one by one until every house was dark and quiet. The moon rose above the bay and shone a silver path across the water. Somewhere in the woods an owl hooted, 'Tooo-hooo, tooo-hooo.'

And then, in the distance, came a strange sound. Far away at first, coming nearer and nearer, a whirring, whirling, clackety noise, louder and louder.

In the little houses and cottages of the village, one or two people stirred in their sleep. The Deggas baby whimpered in her cot, a dog barked, and a prowling cat fled beneath a hollybush in alarm. But no one awoke and looked through a window. Which was very lucky for Sir Benjamin Bathbun and Thumper. For they were flying over the village in a helicopter and Sir Benjamin was in fear and trembling that the villagers would awake and see them.

The pilot followed the railway line to the siding, and, in a minute or two, was hovering low over the shed.

'Down you go, Thumper, you first,' commanded Sir Benjamin. Down a rope slid Thumper, closely followed by Sir Benjamin. Thumper tackled the lock on the shed door.

'Oh dear me. I don't like this at all,' said Sir Benjamin, nervously looking over his shoulders. 'I think we'll return to Bathbun Towers, Thumper.'

'What?' cried Thumper, 'without the engine?

Think of it, sir. Standing in your barn, shiny and bright, just as you've always wanted. It'll look a treat there, sir.'

'Oh yes, you are right, Thumper,' nodded Sir Benjamin. 'Yes, I must have that engine. I don't care how I get her. Hurry up, Thumper, someone may come.'

The door of the shed swung open. Sir Benjamin gave a gasp of delight as he saw the little engine standing there in the moonlight. He released the brakes and they pushed her out on to the lines. Working quickly they fastened her with grappling hooks on chains which the pilot lowered down to them. Awakened from sleep, Forester felt quite bewildered. Whatever was happening to her?

'That's it. Haul away,' ordered Sir Benjamin. In a few moments he and Thumper were back in the helicopter.

'Off we go,' cried Sir Benjamin triumphantly. Up and up rose the helicopter, the little engine slung beneath it, up and away from the village, across the woods and over the hill, heading for Bathbun Towers.

'I'm flying,' thought Forester. 'I'm a flying engine.'

Before the night was over the little engine stood in Sir Benjamin's big barn.

'There, what did I say, sir?' asked Thumper proudly. 'Doesn't she look just right there?'

Oh indeed, Thumper,' agreed Sir Benjamin. 'But I must send Mr Bubbus and Mr Deggas the money tomorrow, because I am not a bad man. I *must* pay for the engine, you know.'

'As you say, sir,' said Thumper. 'Good night.'

With a final glance at Forester they went to bed, and the lights went out in Bathbun Towers.

Next morning, after breakfast, Mr Bubbus walked to the siding, looking forward to the day. He saw the door unlocked and open.

'Funny,' he thought. 'I'm sure we locked that last night.'

He peered into the shed. He had a dreadful shock. *It was empty*. Mr Bubbus searched about wildly. He ran back down the siding. He looked along the bay. The railway lines curved, glinting in the early morning sun, but there was no little engine upon them anywhere.

Mr Bubbus ran back to Station House. Mr Deggas had just arrived.

'Good morning, good morning, good morning,' he greeted his friend cheerily.

'It isn't a g-g-good morning,' panted Mr Bubbus breathlessly. 'Forester has gone.'

'Gone where?' asked Mr Deggas.

'Gone, vanished, disappeared,' puffed Mr Bubbus, falling into a chair. 'She's not in the shed, she's not anywhere.'

'She must be somewhere,' said Mr Deggas reasonably. 'Have you looked?'

'I've looked *everywhere*,' said Mr Bubbus indignantly. He was now feeling rather bad-tempered about the whole thing.

Mr Deggas went to see for himself while Mr Bubbus recovered his breath. When he returned he had a very serious face.

'You are right. She has completely disappeared,' he stated.

'Of course she has. I told you so,' said Mr Bubbus impatiently. 'My opinion is that she has been stolen.'

'Yes. We must go to the police at once,' declared Mr Deggas.

They hurried to the cottage of PC Rose and told him the whole story. PC Rose walked down to the station to view the scene of the crime.

'Hmmm-hmmmm. Yes. She's disappeared right enough,' he nodded. 'But how? How could someone steal a heavy old engine?'

'You tell us. You find her. You're the policeman,' cried Mr Bubbus, red-faced and furious.

While PC Rose hunted about for clues, Mr Bubbus and Mr Deggas organised a search-party.

Everyone from the village joined in. They combed the fields and woods, looked into every shed and garage, peered into every hole and corner, but there was no sign of the little engine. Poppy burst into tears.

'Oh dear, Forester has gone for-forever,' she sobbed.

'An engine can't vanish in thin air. She's somewhere and we'll find her,' said Mr Deggas determinedly.

Poppy dried her eyes. Sadly they put up a sign which said STATION CLOSED. Passengers turned away disappointed and the two gay carriages stood on the rails, lonely and waiting.

'This is a sad day,' sighed Mr Bubbus.

'Don't despair, old friend. We'll find Forester, you'll see,' said Mr Deggas comfortingly.

'I hope so. I hope so,' muttered Mr Bubbus darkly.

Next morning the postman brought a parcel to Station House. Mr Bubbus cut the string and tore open the wrappings. The parcel was full of money and there was a note inside.

For the engine (it said)
Thank you.

'Well,' gasped Mr Bubbus. 'Well, upon my word.'

He could think of nothing more to say. He ran to the Deggas house and opened the parcel before the astonished eyes of the Deggas family.

'Cooo,' exclaimed Ambrose and Poppy and the twins.

'Money,' said Peterkin.

The babies gurgled and Mr and Mrs Deggas just stared. Mr Bubbus read the note aloud.

'We could buy another engine with that money,' suggested Ambrose.

'No, no, it wouldn't be the same,' protested Poppy, and the others agreed.

'Come to think of it,' said Mr Deggas slowly, 'Forester wasn't really and truly ours. We didn't buy her, we just found her.'

'That's true,' nodded Mr Bubbus. 'I never thought of that before. Oh deary me. What shall we do?'

'No problem. There is only one thing to do,' said Mr Deggas. 'We must find Forester and give this money back. Then we must save up and buy her so that she *will* really and truly be our very own.'

'Agreed,' said the others.

'How shall we begin?' asked Mr Bubbus.

'We must all have a good think,' said Mr Deggas. Silence fell as everyone thought and thought.

Chapter Six

The first clue

At Bathbun Towers, Sir Benjamin was becoming very nervous. At first he had spent all his time in the barn, gazing admiringly at Forester.

'Beautiful, beautiful,' he breathed, walking round her time and time again.

But Bathbun Towers was open for everyone to come in and see his collection of engines and to ride on his model railway. Sir Benjamin had a horrid thought.

'Suppose someone comes in and recognises Forester,' he said to Thumper. 'I'll have to hide her, that's what I'll do.'

'I have a better idea. Let's paint her a different colour and change the number and everything,' suggested Thumper.

'Oh dear me, no. That would never do. No, no,

she must stay as she is,' protested Sir Benjamin.

'Well then, let's cover her over and *pretend* she's being painted,' went on Thumper.

Sir Benjamin thought this was a grand idea, so the little engine was covered with a large canvas sheet and a low rope fence was looped around her to keep people away. Sir Benjamin propped a notice saying KEEP AWAY UNDER REPAIR in front of the canvas and stepped back satisfied.

When the crowds had gone at the end of the day, Sir Benjamin would return alone to the barn, pull aside the canvas and look at Forester, gleaming green, brasswork shining, and sigh happily to himself.

Days passed by and Sir Benjamin began to feel safe again. One fine morning a big BBC van arrived at the gates of Bathbun Towers.

'We are making a film for television,' Sir Benjamin was told. 'May we come in and film your engines?'

'Of course, of course, with pleasure,' said Sir Benjamin delightedly. 'Come in.'

He showed them his model engines, then took them into the barn.

'There you are.'

'What a wonderful collection,' exclaimed the producer admiringly. 'And what have we here, under this canvas?'

'Oh, er, just an old engine being mended,' said Sir Benjamin hastily, going pink in the face. 'Would you like to film my model railway? I'll drive the engine myself.'

'Great idea, great,' enthused the producer.

When the camera-men had finished in the barn, they trundled the cameras to the garden and Sir Benjamin drove the tiny train, its coaches laden with passengers, from the little station by the apple trees, through the vegetable garden, through the rhubarb, round the lake and back to the station. Everyone, including Sir Benjamin, smiled and waved at the camera as they chugged past, and they all enjoyed themselves hugely.

'Very successful, Thumper,' said Sir Benjamin later. 'Now we must wait to see ourselves on television. It will be very interesting.'

And indeed it *was* very interesting, especially to one family who happened to be watching the programme that night.

In the evening, after a long day of searching for the missing engine and finding nothing, everyone returned home, sad and disappointed.

'I think I'll have to ask the town police to come and help,' said PC Rose. 'A steam engine just vanishes. It's a real mystery we have here.'

Mr Bubbus went home to Station House. He made himself some supper, but didn't eat very much. He felt so upset.

Mr Deggas sat and read his paper while the twins and Ambrose and Poppy watched television.

Suddenly Ambrose gave a shout.

'Look, Dad,' he cried. 'Bathbun Towers, you know, over the hill. He has some super engines there.'

Mr Deggas lowered his paper and looked at the screen. He saw the tiny model engines set out in neat rows, on tables and shelves. He saw the real engines in the big barn. He saw the model train packed with waving holiday-makers, chugging its way around the garden, with Sir Benjamin at the engine.

Mr Deggas dropped his paper on the floor and leaped from his chair.

'Great heavens!' he cried. 'Benjamin Bathbun.'

His children gazed at him in astonishment and Mrs Deggas ran in from the kitchen, a look of alarm on her face.

'What is it?' she asked anxiously. 'What is wrong?'

'B-B-Benjamin BBBBathbun,' stuttered her husband. 'There, there, that's the one.'

He pointed wildly at the television set.

'Which one? What do you mean?' questioned Mrs Deggas.

'The man who came that day and wanted to buy our engine. He was there, on the screen, Sir Benjamin Bathbun. I saw his face quite clearly,' explained Mr Deggas excitedly.

'Dad, do you think Sir Benjamin has taken Forester?' asked Ambrose.

'Did you see, in the barn, one engine was covered with a big cloth?' said Poppy. 'Do you think that could be *our* engine?'

'My word, we must look into this,' said Mr Deggas. 'At once. Come on, you two, whatever your names are, come with me.'

Delighted as it was almost bedtime, Ambrose and Poppy followed their father hastily down to Station House while the twins and Peterkin burst into tears because they were left behind.

Mr Bubbus was very surprised to see them and when they all started talking at once, he became very confused.

'One at a time,' he begged. 'One at a time.'

Soon he heard the whole story, of seeing the engines at Bathbun Towers, one covered over in a very mysterious manner, and of Mr Deggas recognising Sir Benjamin on the television screen.

'Knew him at once,' said Mr Deggas. 'Saw him clearly. It's him right enough. The one who wanted to have our little engine.'

'Then we must go there right away,' urged Mr Bubbus. 'Go and fetch PC Rose.'

'Wait. We must be very clever about this,' warned Mr Deggas. 'We may be wrong. We must go carefully until we know for certain.'

'Yes, yes, you are right,' agreed Mr Bubbus.

'We must make a plan,' said Mr Deggas. 'Tomorrow Ambrose and Poppy will be the detectives. They must go to Bathbun Towers and see for themselves.'

'Why can't we go?' asked Mr Bubbus.

'Because Sir Benjamin would know us,' explained Mr Deggas.

'Of course. How clever of you,' said his friend.

'Then we'll decide what to do next,' continued Mr Deggas.

Ambrose and Poppy were so excited about the next day, they could hardly sleep that night. They were ready and waiting, bouncing about in the back of the Deggas car, long before Mr Bubbus came hurrying up the lane from Station House. They purred away from the village, up the hill and down, through the town and out again to where Bathbun Towers stood alone behind high grey walls.

'Now you two, here is the money to go in,' instructed Mr Deggas. 'Have a good look round, but take care.'

'Yes, do be careful, children,' begged Mr Bubbus. 'Sir Benjamin may be a desperate criminal.'

'Oh good,' said Ambrose. 'Come on, Poppy. I'll look after you.'

'I'm not frightened,' protested Poppy, but she had a very fluttery feeling in her tummy.

Mr Bubbus and Mr Deggas sat in the car outside the walls, waiting.

'We must disguise ourselves in case Sir Benjamin comes out or looks over the wall,' said Mr Deggas.

Mr Bubbus put on a pair of sunglasses and

turned his jacket collar up and Mr Deggas stuck on the false moustache he'd thought to bring with him and hid behind his newspaper. He tore two holes in the pages so he could peep through and see what was going on.

Ambrose and Poppy paid for their tickets at the gate and entered the gardens of Bathbun Towers. Threading their way through the crowds, they made straight for the barn. Holding hands, they walked breathlessly inside. What would they find there?

Chapter Seven

Ambrose to the rescue

There were a few people in the barn, wandering around admiring the engines.

'Oh,' exclaimed Ambrose. 'Look at that, Poppy.'

He was about to dart away, but Poppy caught hold of his sleeve.

'Come *on*. We've something to do,' she hissed giving him a look.

'Oh yes, I nearly forgot,' said Ambrose apologetically.

There was no one standing near the canvas-covered engine with its notice KEEP AWAY UNDER REPAIR.

'There it is. What do you think is under there?' murmured Ambrose quietly.

'I'm sure it's our engine,' whispered Poppy. 'Go on, Ambrose, have a peep.'

Ambrose looked round carefully. No one was watching them.

'Go *on*,' urged Poppy.

Ambrose stepped quickly over the rope fence. He edged his way to the corner and gently lifted the canvas, bending and peering underneath. He glanced up, grinning triumphantly.

'It's here. It's ours. It's Forester,' he whispered gleefully.

'Oh Ambrose,' gasped Poppy. 'Hide quickly. Someone is coming.' Hastily her brother wriggled under the canvas and lay still. Poppy stood where she was, trying to look as if nothing was the matter. It was Thumper approaching.

'Now, young lady,' he growled. 'What are you doing here?'

'Just l-l-l-looking,' stammered Poppy.

'Nothing to see here. Move along now,' said

Thumper, standing in front of the notice, and rocking on his heels.

Slowly Poppy moved towards the open door. Under the canvas Ambrose lay, feeling rather warm, his heart banging away.

'I'll wait until it's quiet and then I'll slip out,' he thought to himself.

Poppy didn't like to leave her brother behind but she was a sensible little girl, so she made her way back to the gates and told Mr Bubbus and Mr Deggas what had happened. They were overjoyed to hear that their little engine had been found.

'Well now,' declared Mr Deggas. 'We must go in at once and tell Sir Benjamin Bathbun that the game is up.'

'Poor Ambrose under all that heavy canvas,' sympathised Mr Bubbus, who had a very kind heart.

Paying at the gate, they entered the gardens of Bathbun Towers and quickly Poppy led the way to the big barn. There was no sign of Thumper.

'Oh good, that man has gone,' Poppy breathed with relief. She ran to the covered engine.

'Come out, Ambrose,' she said. 'You are safe now.'

She lifted the canvas but Ambrose was not there.

'He's gone,' she gasped.

Mr Bubbus and Mr Deggas searched all round but there was no sign of Ambrose.

'Oh dear, poor Ambrose, what shall we do?' asked Poppy, almost in tears.

'Follow me,' said Mr Deggas and set off for the house with determined steps, and Mr Bubbus and Poppy trotted behind.

When Ambrose heard Poppy move away, he lay listening. After a few minutes, he carefully lifted the edge of the canvas and peeped out. He could see the two big black boots of Thumper, so he let the canvas drop and waited again. Presently he heard footsteps moving away. Once more he peeped out. Thumper had gone and there was no one about.

'Hooray,' thought Ambrose to himself. He wriggled free and jumped to his feet. He felt a heavy hand on his shoulder and a gruff voice said,

'Aha, caught you, young man. What were you doing under there, hey?' Ambrose nearly jumped out of his skin with fright.

'Come with me,' ordered Thumper and marched Ambrose to the house where they met Sir Benjamin Bathbun in the hall.

'What is this?' he asked, surprised.

'Caught this lad messing about with the covered engine,' explained Thumper.

'And what were you doing there? It said to keep away. My engine is being repaired,' said Sir Benjamin.

'It's not your engine. It's *our* engine,' declared Ambrose indignantly.

'What, what, what's all this?' stuttered Sir Benjamin. 'What's that he's saying?'

At that moment, Mr Deggas, Mr Bubbus and Poppy came in at the open front door.

'He's saying that you have stolen our engine,' cried Mr Deggas in ringing tones.

Ambrose was delighted to see them, but Sir Benjamin's face turned purple and Thumper went white.

'I—you—I mean what?' stammered Sir Benjamin. 'Who are you?'

'Explain yourself, sir. We know all about you,' said Mr Deggas, whipping off his false moustache.

'Yes, we know you,' echoed Mr Bubbus, removing his dark glasses. Sir Benjamin Bathbun recognised the two. He collapsed into a chair.

'You stole our engine,' repeated Mr Deggas.

'I'm going to fetch a policeman this very minute,' announced Mr Bubbus.

'No, no, please, not that,' begged Sir Benjamin. 'I'm not a bad man, really I'm not. Please let me explain.'

He told them the whole story, how for so many years he'd searched everywhere for an 0–4–0 goods engine.

'When I saw Forester, I had to have her,' he confessed. 'I know I did wrong to take her away but I sent you the money for her the next day.'

'We don't want money. We want our engine because we *love* her,' said Mr Deggas.

'How did you get her here?' asked Ambrose curiously.

'Yes, how?' repeated Poppy.

'We used a helicopter,' said Sir Benjamin, mopping his brow.

'A helicopter, of course! We should have thought of that,' said Mr Deggas. 'Upon my word, a helicopter!'

'Here is your money,' said Mr Bubbus, handing

it to Sir Benjamin. 'What do you think, Mr Deggas? Shall I go for a policeman?'

By now, Ambrose and Poppy felt quite sorry for Sir Benjamin sitting quaking in the chair. They had a quiet chat with Mr Bubbus and Mr Deggas, while Sir Benjamin and Thumper waited fearfully.

'Well, these two kind children don't want me to fetch a policeman,' announced Mr Bubbus at last. 'But we must have our engine back *at once*.' Greatly relieved, Sir Benjamin jumped to his feet.

'I promise you I'll send her back tomorrow,' he declared. 'I'm very sorry I took Forester because I can see, like me, you really love steam engines. May I come and see her sometimes?'

Mr Bubbus and Mr Deggas, who were very kind-hearted and could not be cross for long, looked at each other and nodded their heads. They all walked back to the barn and Thumper pulled the canvas away. The little engine stood there, shiny and bright and everyone smiled to see her. Except Sir Benjamin, who had a tear in his eye as he promised once more she would be safely back at Station House next day.

Merrily Mr Bubbus, Mr Deggas, Ambrose and Poppy drove home to the village where everyone was waiting anxiously to hear the news. A great cheer went up when they heard Forester had been found safe and sound.

PC Rose felt he should go and arrest Sir Benjamin Bathbun and Thumper immediately. But Mr Bubbus and Mr Deggas shook their heads firmly.

'He is not a bad man,' excused Mr Bubbus. 'He loves steam engines like we do and I'm afraid he loved our little Forester too much. He is very sorry now.'

PC Rose was rather sad about this as he hadn't arrested anyone for a very long time, but everyone else went happily to bed that night, eagerly looking forward to the next day.

Chapter Eight

The end of the story

They were waiting on the pavements early next morning for Forester to arrive. Some of the boys and girls had little flags ready to wave and the Deggas baby banged a red windmill on the side of her pram.

Mr Bubbus had the station swept and tidy and Ambrose, Poppy, the twins and Peterkin cleaned the windows of the two carriages and polished the door handles, so that everything would be spick and span when the little engine was back on the lines. Time ticked by and all eyes were gazing anxiously up the hill. Mr Deggas looked at his watch several times.

'Oh dear, when *is* she coming?' asked Peterkin wearily.

'I hope Sir Benjamin Bathbun is not going to

play a trick on us,' said Mr Bubbus.

'No, no, no, no,' said Mr Deggas. 'He won't let us down.'

At that very moment, in the distance, a rumbling sound was heard. A buzz of excitement went round the villagers as over the hill lumbered a low-loader carrying Forester, apple-green, brass-work gleaming, as neat and trim as ever. Slowly, slowly down the hill to the village, nearer and nearer she came.

'Hooray,' cheered the crowd. 'Hooray, hooray.'

Hats were raised in the air and flags waved. Mr Bubbus had tears in his eyes and Mr Deggas blew his nose loudly in his clean white handkerchief. They were so happy to see the little engine home again.

She was driven past Station House to a place

where she could be lifted on to the lines by the two cranes which had come with her. Thumper was there, ordering everyone about, but there was no sign of Sir Benjamin Bathbun.

He had stayed in Bathbun Towers, Thumper informed them. Behind closed curtains, because he couldn't bear to watch Forester being taken away. Mr Bubbus and Mr Deggas 'tut tutted' sympathetically.

At last, after being swung through the air and bumped about rather a lot, Forester stood on the lines. The cranes and the low-loader went away.

'Now, to work,' said Mr Deggas briskly. 'We'll coal her and water her, then off we go, trips around the bay.'

'Business as usual,' cried Mr Bubbus with a smile.

'Hooray,' cheered the children.

Forester was made ready and coupled to the carriages. Mr Bubbus and Mr Deggas put on their hats and jumped merrily on to the footplate.

'Here we go,' laughed Mr Bubbus.

But *nothing* happened. Absolutely *nothing*.

Mr Bubbus pulled this lever and pushed that one, but Forester, apart from one little gasp, neither moved nor made a sound.

'What's the problem?' asked Mr Deggas.

'I don't know,' confessed Mr Bubbus. 'I'll have another try.'

The Deggas family watched worriedly but no matter what Mr Bubbus did, Forester stood silent and still. After a long time, Mr Bubbus pushed his hat back on his head and sighed.

'It's no good. I can't make her go.'

'I expect it's all that's happened to her,' said Mr Deggas. 'Hauled through the air by helicopter, left in strange places, bumped about on a low-loader, and dumped about by cranes.'

'You are right,' agreed Mr Bubbus. 'After all, Forester isn't young, poor thing.'

Everyone gazed sadly at her standing there. Thumper was nearby, watching.

'Shall I fetch Sir Benjamin to have a look at the engine?' he suggested. 'He really is an expert on old engines, you know. He may be able to help.'

'A good idea. Why not?' said Mr Deggas at once, and everyone agreed. 'Come along, I'll take you to Bathbun Towers and we'll bring Sir Benjamin back.'

Off they went and the crowds drifted home. But Ambrose, Poppy, the twins and Peterkin stayed and kept Mr Bubbus company. They sat in Station House playing 'I Spy' and games like that, every now and again glancing out of the window to see if Mr Deggas was returning with Sir Benjamin.

At last Peterkin shouted triumphantly,

'I spy Daddy coming down the hill!'

Everyone dashed out to meet Mr Deggas. Sir Benjamin Bathbun was sitting next to him and Thumper was in the back seat.

'Here we are, here we are, no problem,' cried Mr Deggas and in less than a minute, Sir Benjamin Bathbun was on the footplate of Forester, giving her a thorough examination.

Mr Bubbus, Mr Deggas and the children stood on the platform watching anxiously.

'Hmmmmm,' said Sir Benjamin thoughtfully. 'Hmmmm hmm. Aha. A-haaaa.'

'What is it? What do you think?' enquired the others.

'Well now, let me see. The thingummy-jig here needs a spot of grease, the thingummy-bob there is rather loose. The what's-its-name is out of place and the who-d'you-call-it is missing altogether. I think that seems to be the trouble.'

'Can you mend her?' asked Mr Bubbus.

'Of course. I won't be long,' said Sir Benjamin confidently. And sure enough, presently Forester gave a great long sigh and a shudder. A puff of steam rose into the air.

'Shuff chuff,' she said. 'Shuff, chuff.'

'There, as good as new,' declared Sir Benjamin, stepping down and wiping his greasy hands on his hanky.

'Oh thank you, thank you so much,' said Mr Bubbus gratefully and everyone joined in.

'Come for a ride with us,' invited Mr Deggas.

'Glad to, delighted,' said Sir Benjamin.

Mr Bubbus blew a great blast on the whistle.

'Whoooo-hoooo.'

Everyone in the village heard it and knew that Forester was fit and well again. In a few minutes the carriages were full and they were off. Round the curving, gleaming lines of the bay rolled Forester, clickety click, clickety clack.

'Shuff chuff,' she said. 'Shuff chuff.'

Later Mr Bubbus and Mr Deggas put their heads together and had a little chat.

'My friend and I are so grateful to you for helping us,' said Mr Deggas to Sir Benjamin. 'We wonder if you would like to come down here sometimes and drive our little engine?'

'We know you love her too,' added Mr Bubbus.

'How very kind of you,' said Sir Benjamin. 'I would be very happy to drive Forester sometimes, indeed I would.'

So it was arranged.

The summer days passed by. Holiday-makers came and went and everyone wanted a trip on the little train around the bay. Mr Bubbus and Mr Deggas were as busy as could be.

Two or three times a week Thumper drove Sir Benjamin over from Bathbun Towers and Sir Benjamin put on his driver's hat, took his place on the footplate and happily drove the engine all day.

This was a splendid arrangement as it gave time for Mr Bubbus and Mr Deggas to do some shopping and have their hair cut and things like that.

When at last the wonderful summer came to an end and the holiday-makers had gone home and the leaves were beginning to change colour, Mr Bubbus and Mr Deggas counted up all the money they had made.

They had enough to buy Forester and make her their very own. This made everyone very happy and one fine autumn afternoon, they had a party on the station to celebrate. Tables and chairs were set out on the platform, tea and lemonade were served through the kitchen window, Mrs Deggas and the ladies handed round the sandwiches and cakes they had made. Everyone was there including Sir Benjamin and Thumper and presently Mr Deggas called for silence.

'Ladies and gentlemen, boys and girls,' he said. 'A toast to our very own steam engine Forester and to the Bubbus and Deggas Railway Co.'

They stood and raised their cups and glasses.

'Forester,' they said. 'The Bubbus and Deggas Railway Co.'

'Three cheers for Forester, three cheers for the Railway Co., three cheers for us,' cried Mr Bubbus who was very excited by it all. He threw his driver's hat into the air.

'Hooray, hooray, hooray,' the cheers echoed across the bay.

Forester stood on the lines, apple-green, brass gleaming, the two gay carriages behind her. She was content.

'Shuff chuff,' she said. 'Shuff chuff.'

More Beaver Books

We hope you have enjoyed this Beaver Book. Here are some of the other titles:

Rhyme Time Over two hundred poems specially chosen by Barbara Ireson to introduce younger readers to the pleasures of reading verse. This lively collection is illustrated throughout

Wilberforce the Whale Leslie Coleman's story about a young and jolly whale, Wilberforce, who sets off with his two young friends Melody the shrimp and Nelson the crab, on a visit to his Aunty Barnacle in Scotland. An amusing story for younger readers with illustrations by John Laing

All the Fun of the Fair When the fair comes to town, Kay, Rory and Gerald have amusing adventures with a fortune-teller, a lady bareback rider, the elephant boy and the baby elephant who loves apples; written by Dorothy Clewes for younger readers

Snail Tale A charming story about a snail and his friend, an ant, who got off on a journey; written by Avi and illustrated by Tom Kindron

The Tail of the Trinosaur Charles Causley's splendidly funny verse story about a prehistoric beast which comes to England from the Amazon jungle; with illustrations by Jill Gardiner

Animal Quiz Johnny Morris, universally known and loved for his television programme, Animal Magic, has created a picture quiz book about all sorts of animals, fish and birds, full of fun and fact for all the family

New Beavers are published every month and if you would like the *Beaver Bulletin* – which gives all the details – please send a large stamped envelope to:

Beaver Bulletin
The Hamlyn Group
Astronaut House
Feltham
Middlesex TW14 9AR

362752